HISTORY CORNER

Popcorn

D0230939

Tudors

Alice Harman

Explore the world with **Popcorn** - your complete first non-fiction library.

Look out for more titles in the Popcorn range. All books have the same format of simple text and striking images. Text is carefully matched to the pictures to help readers to identify and understand key vocabulary. www.waylandbooks.co.uk/popcorn

Published in 2015 by Wayland
Copyright © Wayland 2015

Wayland
Hachette Children's Books
338 Euston Road
London NW1 3BH

Wayland Australia
Level 17/207 Kent Street
Sydney NSW 2000

Produced for Wayland by
White-Thomson Publishing Ltd
www.wtpub.co.uk
+44 (0)843 208 7460

Editor: Alice Harman
Designer: Clare Nicholas
Picture researcher: Alice Harman
Series consultant: Kate Ruttle
Design concept: Paul Cherrill

British Library Cataloguing in Publication Data
Harman, Alice.
  Tudors. -- (History corner)(Popcorn)
  1. Great Britain--History--Tudors, 1485-1603--Juvenile
literature. 2. Great Britain--Social conditions--16th
century--Juvenile literature. 3. Great Britain--Social
life and customs--16th century--Juvenile literature.
I. Title II. Series
942'.05-dc23

ISBN: 978 0 7502 9526 0

Wayland is a division of Hachette Children's Books,
an Hachette UK company.
www.hachette.co.uk

Printed and bound in China

Picture/illustration credits: Alamy: The Art Collection
14; Peter Bull 23; Stefan Chabluk 4; Corbis: Steven Vidler/
Eurasia Press cover, John Miller/Robert Harding World
Imagery/Corbis 10, Heritage Images 11/12; Getty:
Severino Barald 8, Hulton Archive 13, Bridgeman Art
Library 17; Mary Evans: Illustrated London News Ltd 16;
Shutterstock: Padmayogini 20; Topfoto: Fotomas 15/21,
The British Library/HIP 19; Wikimedia 1/9, 2/6/22, 5/22,
7/22, 18, 22.

Every effort has been made to clear copyright.
Should there be any inadvertent omission,
please apply to the publisher for rectification.

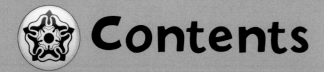

Contents

Who were the Tudors?

The Tudors were a family who ruled England more than 500 years ago. People who lived in England at this time are also called Tudors.

The Tudor family ruled England for around 120 years.

EUROPE

SCOTLAND

North Sea

Atlantic Ocean

IRELAND

Irish Sea

York

ENGLAND

Norwich

WALES

Pembroke

Bristol

Oxford London

FRANCE

English Channel

Tudor England and Wales

Towns/cities

Henry VII was the first Tudor king of England. He became king by winning a battle against Richard III, who was the king before him.

Henry VII is holding the Tudor Rose, the sign of the Tudor family.

Kings and queens

Henry VIII was the second king from the Tudor family. He had six wives. He wanted to have a son, to rule England after him.

Henry VIII liked to wear expensive clothes that showed his wealth and power.

Elizabeth I was queen for 44 years. She never got married or had children. She was the last person from the Tudor family to rule England.

Elizabeth I told people to travel around the world and find new lands.

Town and country

London was the largest Tudor city. People moved there from the countryside to find work. The streets were often crowded and smelly.

People threw their rubbish, dirty water and toilet waste into the street!

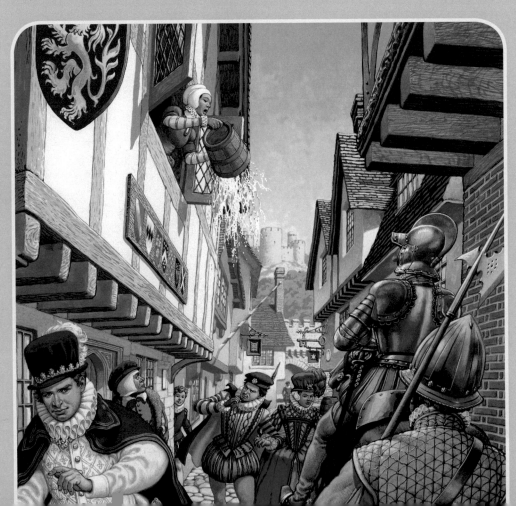

Most people in Tudor England lived in small villages in the countryside. Rich people often had homes in the city and the countryside.

This painting shows wealthy guests at a wedding in a village near London.

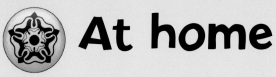

At home

Most Tudor houses were made out of wood and a mixture of clay, sand and animal dung. This mixture is called daub.

These houses in the English town of Lavenham were built more than 500 years ago, in Tudor times.

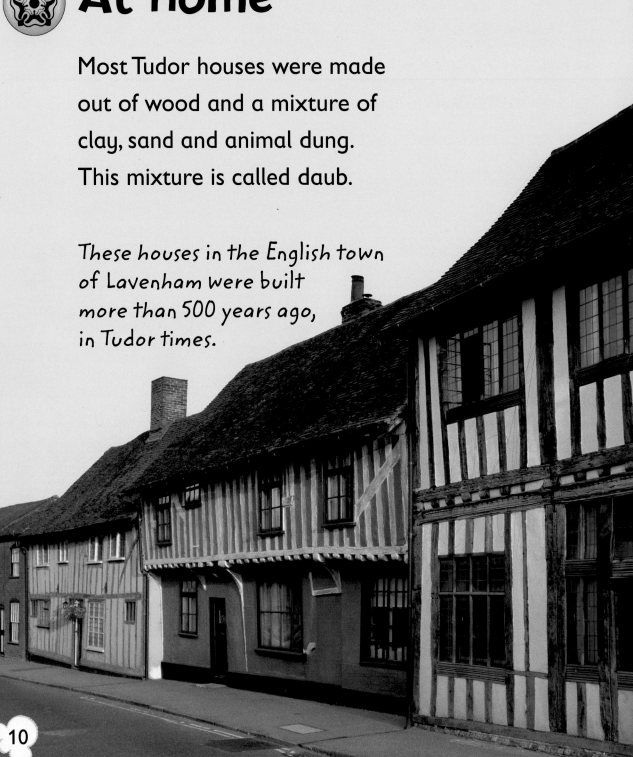

Very rich people had huge country houses. The rooms were decorated with paintings, carpets and expensive furniture.

Rich families ate meals and sat together in the Great Hall.

Large pictures made of fabric were hung on the walls for decoration. They are called tapestries.

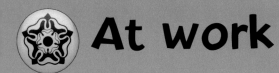

At work

Many people in the towns worked
to make goods such as cloth,
soap and glass. People worked
for up to 15 hours a day.

Dyed cloth was
soaked in wee!
This stopped the
colour coming out
when the cloth
was washed.

These workers
are dyeing a
piece of cloth
to make it red.

Most Tudors worked on farms.
These farms were owned by rich
families. People were not paid
much money for doing farm work.

This Tudor drawing shows how men
and women worked together in the fields.

Children

Tudor parents often had big families. Over a third of all children died before the age of 16. Most girls got married when they were 12 to 14 years old.

Older children in rich families were dressed like adults.

Most poor children did not go to school. Some boys went to free schools, if they passed an exam. Rich boys and some rich girls had classes at home with a teacher.

In class, boys were only allowed to speak in Latin. Latin is a very old language.

In the classroom, children sat together on long benches. They didn't have desks.

 Food

Rich people sometimes had large dinner parties. They served many expensive dishes, such as meats and sweet pies.

At Tudor feasts, people ate swans and peacocks!

While they ate, guests were entertained by singers and dancers wearing costumes.

Servants prepared all the food that rich people ate. They did not eat this food themselves. Servants and other poor people mostly ate vegetable soup, porridge and bread.

Servants hung pots over the fire to cook soups, sauces and other dishes.

Clothes

Wealthy Tudor people wore clothes made from expensive fabrics, such as silk and lace. Their clothes were decorated with gold and silver.

Only the Tudor royal family were allowed to wear purple clothes.

Rich Tudor men and women wore huge collars called ruffs, made of white lace.

Most people owned only one set of
clothes. They were made at home
from wool or linen. Women wore
long dresses, and men wore tunics
over short trousers.

Women never wore trousers. They sat with
both legs on one side when they rode horses.

Fun and leisure

Many people loved to watch plays. Actors travelled around England to perform plays in different towns and villages.

William Shakespeare was a famous Tudor playwright. He wrote 38 plays.

Shakespeare's plays are still performed today in countries around the world.

Lots of Tudors played football and tennis. These sports had different rules to the ones we use today. Some sports were banned so that people would play less and work more.

Rich and poor people enjoyed bowling. Players threw a ball to knock down pieces of wood.

Name that Tudor!

On this page, you can see pictures of all the Tudor kings and queens. The king at the top was the first Tudor to rule England. The queen at the bottom was the last.

In this book, you've read about two kings and one queen from the Tudor family.

Go back and try to find their names. Then match the right name to the right picture on this page.

The names are in the panel below, but they may not be in the right order.

Henry VIII

Elizabeth I

Henry VII

King _____?_____

King _____?_____

King Edward VI

Queen Mary I

Queen _____?_____

Make a Tudor Rose

The Tudor Rose is the sign of the Tudor royal family. Tudor kings and queens often held Tudor Roses in paintings.

You will need:
- one piece of card
- four sheets of coloured paper (red, white, green and yellow)
- scissors · glue stick

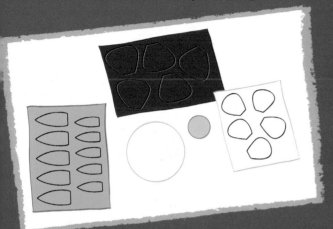

1. Cut a circle out of the card, and a smaller circle out of the yellow paper. Draw shapes on the coloured paper, as shown in this picture. Cut them all out.

2. Glue the larger green leaves evenly around the edge of the circle of card. Then stick the red petals onto the centre of the card circle, so that the green leaves show through the spaces between the red petals.

3. Stick on the small green leaves and the white petals, in the same pattern as in Step 2. Glue the yellow circle on top. Now you have your own Tudor Rose!

Visit our website to download larger, printable templates for this project.

www.waylandbooks.co.uk/popcorn

Glossary

ban to stop people from doing something

clay a type of earth that is used for making and building things

collar the part of a shirt or coat that fits around the neck

desk a table used for writing and working

dung the poo of large animals

lace a thin fabric with a pattern of small holes

linen a type of cloth made from the flax plant

peacock a type of bird; the male bird has bright blue and green feathers

playwright someone who writes plays for people to perform in theatres

royal describes a king or queen, or a member of their family

scar a mark left on someone's skin by an old cut or sore

silk a soft, smooth fabric

swan a large white bird that has a long neck and lives in and around water

tunic a long, loose top with no sleeves

wealthy rich, has a lot of money

wool a warm fabric made from sheep's hair

Index